Firm Foundations

A Parents' Guide
to the Skills
Essential
for Reading
and Writing

Clare Welsh and Lynn Fallaize

This book is dedicated with love to our daughters

Lauren, Samantha, Michelle, Rosalind.

Parents of the future.

First published in Great Britain by Barrington Stoke Ltd,
Sandeman House, 55 High Street, Edinburgh, EH1 1SR

www.barringtonstoke.co.uk

Copyright © 2005 Barrington Stoke

ISBN 1-84299-300-3

Edited by Julia Rowlandson

Illustrations by Lynn Fallaize

Cover design by Kate MacPhee

Typeset by GreenGate Publishing Services, Tonbridge

Printed in Great Britain by The Cromwell Press

Contents

The Theory Bit!

Future historians will look back over the 20th century and wonder at the speed and degree of change we have experienced. Huge technological advances and global communications have had a massive impact on our society. Even within the last 50 years, our lifestyle has altered so much that our great grandparents would barely recognise family life, as we know it now. The dynamics of work, relationships and parenthood were very different, the pace of life was slower and our horizons were not very far away.

Life was certainly not as comfortable as nowadays, and one would be foolish to suggest that everything was rosy in those days. However, there were certain aspects which were good, and which have disappeared, much to our loss.

Families were not distracted from talking to each other by televisions and computers. They congregated together in the warmest rooms in the house during winter rather than living isolated lives in separate bedrooms, as is sadly often the case nowadays. Playing out with friends until dark, or playing games with each other inside, alleviated long hours of boredom for children. There would have been many more opportunities for conversation, and meals were traditionally served round the table where all members of the family could share their daily experiences and offer opinions. In this language-rich and interactive environment, children could be inventive, learn to listen, think, speak and communicate with others and practise other important skills which would help prepare them for formal schooling.

Education was different too; it was often more rigid, and therefore tough for those who found it difficult to learn or conform. Teaching was done with a minimum of resources, often just a blackboard and chalk, and pupils were always under the threat of punishment for poor work or disobedience!

However, then as now, for many children play times and the long lunch hour were welcome breaks from work; wet playtimes were rare and children were bundled out into the playground to 'let off steam' in all weathers.

And it is what went on during those times of play, both at home and at school, that is the interesting part for us and this book. Unwittingly, those children were practising skills which would be invaluable for underpinning the processes of reading and writing. Every day, they were building the foundations for literacy.

They were sharpening skills such as:

- **Visual discrimination**, which is the ability to see differences in things, be it colours, shapes, symbols, (including letters), patterns etc. and which is strengthened by doing puzzles, patterns, sorting, matching, and popular games such as 'Spot the Difference' or 'Odd One Out'.
- **Phonological awareness**, which we now know is a basic requirement for good reading and spelling, through a myriad of rhymes, rhyming skipping games and verbal ditties.
- **Sequencing**, which includes visual (seeing), auditory (hearing) and kinaesthetic (movement), through games such as 'Hopscotch', cards, making patterns and skipping games.

- **Memory**, which includes visual, auditory and sequential (sequencing), and underpins not only learning but all areas of our functioning and which is strengthened by the playing of numerous card games and verbal games such as 'I went to market' or 'Who stole the cookie?'.
- **Fine motor**, through games such as 'Jacks' and 'Cat's Cradle', which promote manual dexterity, which is in turn vital for good pencil control and handwriting.

Sometimes these skills are referred to as 'pre-literacy skills' or 'sub-skills'; that is, children need to have acquired them *before* they are ready to make a success of reading and writing. In fact, most of the old playground games involved using more than one of these skills at the same time, and so were wonderful for promoting all-round development and co-ordination.

Hopefully, we can already see the value these games had for growing children and developing brains. They were the building blocks or foundations upon which future literacy skills were built. Why they were real winners though, was that the children were unaware that they were learning, because, of course, they were learning through *play*.

Nowadays, because of the changes in education, society and advances in technology, children fail to have as much opportunity to practise these skills as they used to.

Children begin literacy during their Reception year at school, and for some, these pre-literacy skills are still not quite finely tuned enough. The 'Literacy Hour' which the government introduced into schools in the late 1980's, has brought a welcome structure to the teaching of reading and writing, but unfortunately leaves little time for children who are struggling with the pace of it to re-visit these skills.

It sometimes seems as if we have forgotten the importance of pre-literacy skills.

The aim of this book, therefore, is two-fold.

Firstly, it is an attempt to identify and explain to parents exactly what these skills are and highlight the importance of them as foundations to a child beginning his literacy career.

And secondly, it will provide parents of young children, or parents of older children who may be struggling with literacy, with a bank of enjoyable activities to play at home.

What Exactly Is Literacy?

Put very simply, literacy is reading and writing. In order for us to understand the importance of helping children prepare for this task, we need to take a very close look at what it consists of and how we learn to do it. We also need to see it through the eyes of the child so we can recognise what a complicated and sometimes baffling process it is.

'Big school', to the children approaching their fifth birthday, is an exciting but often bewildering world. Suddenly, they are cut loose from the protective arm of home and possibly play school and thrust into a world which is not only physically huge but also bombards them with sensory stimulation: sound, actions and visual input. It is a structured day, one full of rules, when they will be set tasks to complete within a specified time. In fact, it is very easy for the less confident child or the child with delayed development, and the child who is already manifesting learning difficulties, to become overwhelmed and fail to grasp the early reading and writing skills.

'Decoding' and 'encoding' are the processes at the heart of literacy. If you think about it, letters are nothing more than *symbols which represent sounds*. They appear to a young child as little squiggles on sheets of paper or on the board, or in books. Sometimes these squiggles are made with a pen and sometimes they are already printed in the book. They are everywhere in the classroom; they are in the cloakrooms, on the walls, on the playhouse door, on colouring books, on the drawers, the desks and even the windows.

Reading is the skill we need in order to make sense of them. It can be taught and it can be learnt.

The chances are that those of you reading this book right now will never remember the time when you couldn't read. In fact for most of us, reading is so automatic that it is easy to assume that it is something which 'just happened', or that we learnt it by some kind of osmosis. And, of course, for the vast majority of us, the ability to read and write **is** something which we do acquire fairly easily, over a period of some years, providing we have sound teaching, motivation and a lot of practice.

Reading and writing, however, has not been necessary to our survival as a species. Various civilisations throughout history have left evidence of their ability to put language into symbols and have left written accounts of their ancient cultures. Think of the hieroglyphics found inside the pyramids of Egypt or other archaeological sites around the world. However, reading and writing was usually the task for only a handful of educated and high status people, such as religious clergy, lawyers, administrators and others. Even in our own country, reading and writing was the domain of relatively few people until only about 130 years ago, when an elementary education was made compulsory for all.

Therefore, it could be argued that there is little intrinsic motivation to read for the average young child. He cannot know to what extent his success at school and therefore often his success in adult life depends on his grasp of literacy. Many of us can testify that there is a great deal of pleasure to be had in reading a good book, but of course nowadays there are television programmes, films and computerised games as alternative pastimes for us all. Parents and pre-school groups can certainly do much to foster the young child's interest in books and there is a huge selection of beautifully illustrated books for children of all ages just waiting to be read in our local bookshops and libraries. A first and vital step towards literacy for any child is for his parents or carers to read stories with him regularly and share their own enthusiasm.

Re-motivating a struggling reader is more difficult. While they are young enough, parents can still share books and read with their children. As they get older, this is less likely to be acceptable. Fortunately, however, there is an increasing number of high interest/low level books available which are written for struggling readers whereby the storyline is age appropriate but the actual text is easier to read. Children of all ages need to feel successful with their reading if they are to be motivated to continue.

There is an ongoing debate as to the most appropriate time to introduce a child to reading and writing. Different countries start their literacy programmes at different ages. For example, many European countries delay literacy until the age of six and concentrate on developing motor, social, life, learning and other foundation skills through play and practical investigation during the first few years in school. Schools in the U.K. usually start to teach literacy in Reception Year, during which time the children have their fifth birthday. Unfortunately, all children do not develop and mature at the same rate, for a variety of reasons. These reasons can include health, gender, inherent physical, cognitive and language developmental rates, social background and environment. So whilst there may be some four year olds who have well advanced pre-literacy skills, and are capable of tackling the task of reading, many are not ready until later. We can accept that our children teeth, walk, talk, and become dry at different ages and yet for the convenience of the education system, we generally impose our own timetable for commencing academic skills.

Although this is not the place to pursue this particular debate, it can be seen that some four or five year olds might not yet be equipped with the skills necessary to make a *confident* start with reading and so be assured of success. The introduction of the 'Literacy Strategy' in 1998 brought a structure to the way schools teach literacy, but its pace is quite fast for some younger learners. Many children and adults need a lot of practice to help them remember new information, or succeed at mastering a new skill. The school timetable is very full and finding adequate time for practice is sometimes difficult for teachers.

But, if children fail to acquire these essential pre-literacy skills, they are going to start off at a disadvantage, and a gap between them and their classmates will appear as they move through their school years.

Our education system statistics reveal that many children struggle to learn to read and write and some never achieve a good level of literacy. Often from the start these children seem unable to make any kind of sense of the written word. Reading becomes an activity which defeats them repeatedly, and one from which they quickly learn to shrink away. It's tough when others seem to be able to do something easily that they find so hard. It gets even tougher when they are required to actually write words and sentences down in their books; if reading was confusing, then writing becomes unfathomable. Worse still, the reading and writing starts to crop up all over their timetable; as they go up the years they need to be able to read and write to do their History, Geography, Science, R.E., P.H.S.E., Design & Technology, and so the list goes on. In our educational culture, good literacy is usually synonymous with academic achievement. Pupils who find literacy difficult will struggle to achieve across the curriculum. No wonder that at some point, many children just shrug their shoulders, or worse, and begin to display bad behaviour, and simply give up on school. It's all too much for them. This insistence on reading and writing, which they find **so** difficult, is causing them to fail on a daily (or hourly) basis. Not one of us puts up with continual failure. We find a way to opt out.

Government statistics reveal that there is a close link between illiteracy and antisocial behaviour in adolescent and adult life. While there are clearly many other contributing factors to this, there can be no doubt that poor literacy skills can lead to a sense of failure academically, low self esteem and a lack of motivation to succeed generally. Sadly, this often results in a feeling of alienation from the mainstream community. It is the responsibility of government, schools, teachers and parents or carers to try to ensure that this does not happen.

There has been a lot of research and media attention in recent times into 'Specific Learning Difficulties', of which 'Dyslexia' is probably the most well known and well documented. It is a complex subject and research indicates that may be as many as 10% of the population are affected by it to some degree or another. Most children who have dyslexic tendencies will benefit from practice in and reinforcement of the basic skills outlined in this book.

We are going to explore the processes involved in reading and writing and the skills which need to be present and working for reading to take place. These skills, or 'sub-skills' as we shall call them, can be identified, focused upon and practised so that they are strengthened. If a child is known to have a weakness in a particular skill, then this might well be a reason for slow progress in literacy. If that skill can be built up and strengthened, it might well prove to be one of the keys which could unlock his potential to read and write.

It is the aim of this book therefore, to help parents who want to be involved in teaching their children to read and write, to see exactly what processes are involved and what skills **anyone** needs to possess before they can begin to unravel the mysteries of the written word.

We are also going to give parents ideas for practical exercises and activities which they can do with their children for fun. By doing this they can either help their young child be ready to read and write, or help them to overcome their difficulties if they are showing signs that they are struggling.

How Do We Learn To Read And Write?

We have already said that most of us cannot remember a time when we could not read or write. But how very different it suddenly is for us if we take a trip abroad to a foreign country. If modern languages were not our strength at school, the likelihood is that even when we visit a close neighbour such as France, Spain or Germany we often feel confused and not a little insecure because we cannot understand the hundreds of written signs on roads, in shops and other public places. And yet at least these countries use the same alphabet as us. At least we might be able to make some kind of attempt to sound out a word or two in an emergency. But let's take a trip further afield, say, to Greece, where the very alphabet is totally different and see how we get on.

The following exercise will help us remember what it's like to be a child; to NOT to be able to read, and it will help us discover what we must do in order to read or write a single word in any language!

Here we are, faced with the Greek alphabet!

α β γ δ ε ζ η θ ι κ λ μ ξ ο π σ τ ν φ χ ψ ω

How do you feel?

Immediately our familiarity (and possibly our confidence) is gone and we find ourselves in exactly the same position as many young children on their first day at school.

But, next, before we have hardly had time to take it all in, we are shown these words, and we are expected to have a go at reading one or two of them …

ιδου! εντανθα εστιν ο κνων

Pause for a moment before reading on and ask yourself, what is the very first thing you need to be able to do to start to work this out?

Most people will say they need to know what sound each letter makes. And that is exactly right. But there are processes which come before even that early step. Firstly, you need to know that we call these symbols, (for that is exactly what they are), 'letters', and a group of letters, which are marked by having a space in between them, is going to be called a 'word', and that most letters on their own mean nothing, while most words do.

You then need to be able to see the *difference* between the letters. If you think about it, there is little difference visually between a 'b' and an 'h', or an 'o' and an 'a', or a 'q' and a 'g'. No wonder we find some children persist in mixing up 'p', 'd', 'b' and 'q'. If we are to read and write some Greek, we need to spot the differences between the letters and also remember which way round they face before going any further.

And now we also need to be sure that we can actually hear the differences between the sounds. Again, for us as adults, we cannot imagine this being difficult, but be assured that if we were learning a non-European language whose sound systems were very different to ours, most of us would struggle greatly. Even with English, some sounds are extremely similar. Take, for example, 'f' and 'th', or 'b' and 'p'. Younger children can find these differences difficult to distinguish in their spoken language which leads to confusion with the written word.

But for now let us assume that the learner has no problems in seeing that all the letters are different, and has very good hearing and can tell the differences between all the sounds. All 24 of them! So now, the only challenge is to commit them all to memory. Consider how many times you would need to go over and over the sounds before you could remember them all. Here, it is worth pointing out that if you were to learn the Greek alphabet by rote, you would then be able to keep referring back to it to remind yourself of some of the letter names. In Greek, as in English, many letter names give a clue to their sound, and this would be a useful way to jog your memory.

Next you need to know how the different sounds blend together. Some languages are more regular than others, and English is one which has a lot of irregularities. For example, we have straightforward blends, such as two consonants, e.g. 'f' and 'l', which says 'fl', but we also have two consonants which can say something completely different, e.g. 's' and 'h' which says 'sh', or 'p' and 'h', 'ph', which makes the same sound as the single letter, 'f'. Again, we need the help of a good teacher to teach us those blends, and then we need a pretty keen memory to remember them for next time.

Incidentally, one thing we have assumed throughout this exercise so far, is that Greek writing starts at the top left hand side of the page, and works down in horizontal lines to the bottom right. As a matter of fact it does, but many non-European languages are written from right to left. So it's a good idea to ascertain where you are starting from.

So now, how close are we to de-ciphering our Greek sentence? We know which side of the page we are starting from, and we can see the differences between the letters. We have remembered what sound each letter makes, and we have even remembered that some letters blend together in certain ways. After this, we should be able to have a go at sounding out a word or two.

And then, AS LONG AS WE UNDERSTAND THEIR MEANING … we are beginning to make sense of the written word.

So now, the next challenge is to write a sentence of our own in Greek. That's a bit more tricky, because it doesn't only involve all the processes above, i.e., knowing the differences between the letters, the sounds, remembering the blends, knowing where to start, but you also have to remember in which order the letters go. You cannot just write them down randomly. And here again memory plays an important part. We must get the order right or our word will either mean something completely different or make no sense at all. For example, 'great' becomes 'grate' when the 'e' is in the wrong place. Or, 'mast' becomes 'mats' when we place the 's' and the 't' in the wrong order. We need to have a lot of practice, and see the words many times so that we can memorise the correct order.

It will always be easier to read than to write an unfamiliar language, as writing involves more processes. Children are usually better at reading than writing at first. Much Chinese and Japanese writing used to be done with a brush, rather than a pen or pencil. Most of us can use a pencil easily, but learning how to make the bristles on the brush do what we want them to do could require a lot of practice. In other words, writing also requires a degree of control over our writing tools, which in turn requires adequate manual dexterity for the task.

But, before we move on, what did that Greek sentence mean?

It was a sentence which could appear in many children's early reading books:

'Look! Here is the dog.'

Let's Look At The Skills

We hope this short exercise has helped you to fully appreciate as a parent the challenge your child faces in acquiring the many different sub-skills which are called into use in order to read or write. Reading is fundamentally the act of translating a coded message into ordinary language – the dictionary calls it '**decoding**'. Once the code is cracked, writing is the act of '**encoding**'- putting spoken language into the written code.

As with most things in life, professionals have built up a whole vocabulary to describe these sub-skills. Although some of you reading this book will be familiar with the 'jargon', many of you may not be, so a brief summary follows of what each skill involves. The activities in 'The Fun Bit!' of this book will be coded with the following symbols to identify the main skill or skills they are practising, so you can target the needs of your own child.

Visual Discrimination Skills

These concern information gathered by the eye and processed by the brain. They include looking at symbols, (or letters), and recognising their unique shape, and being able to see the difference between each one. We use this skill when we tell the difference between red and yellow (colour discrimination), or identify shapes, e.g. a circle from a square. We need it for number recognition as well as reading and writing. It helps us 'Spot the Difference' or find the 'Odd One Out'. Our ancestors used it for survival to identify different shaped and coloured leaves, berries or insects.

Visual orientation is being able to see that letters or symbols can face different directions; left/right or up/down. It is closely related to spatial awareness; that is where we are, or where objects are, in space. This skill is also needed in other school subjects such as Numeracy, Geography, Art, Technology and Science. It helps us when we read a map or follow the instructions for making up flat pack furniture!

Phonological Skills (Auditory)

This is the ability to hear the differences between the sounds each letter or letter combination makes (phonemes). It also involves discerning the various syllables, e.g. 'pic/ture', 'hos/pit/al', and parts of a compound word, e.g. 'dragon/fly' or 'camera/man'. It helps us identify regional accents, hear different tones of voice, and for the hunters of the past it was a necessary skill for hearing the different cries and sounds made by predators and prey.

Sound blending is the process of blending two or more phonemes together in the correct order. We need to be able to say these blends clearly if we are to be understood by our speech, and we need to be able to recognise the two or more phonemes within the word if we are to attempt to spell.

Sequencing

Sequencing can be a visual or an auditory skill, which usually relies on memory. Seeing that letters go in a specific order and hearing that sounds also follow a certain pattern are vital for reading and writing. In life, we use sequencing skills generally to repeat patterns and actions, (such as in music or tap dancing), to do things in a logical way (such as when we get dressed), and to create and bring about progression (such as when we build a house).

Memory

This is such an important component for all areas of academic work, not least learning to read and write. There is Visual Memory, i.e. remembering what you have seen, and Auditory Memory, i.e. remembering what you have heard. In the previous paragraph we talked about a Sequential Memory, which can be Visual or Auditory, which means remembering the order in which you have seen or heard things and finally there is the Kinaesthetic Memory, which is the memory of movement. This can help us considerably when we are trying to spell correctly because the memory of the movement in our hand, which we need to make in order to write a particular word, can be strong. Try writing your signature with your eyes closed; you should be able to do it easily because it is deeply engrained in your kinaesthetic memory. In other words, your hand knows what to do even though your eyes cannot see. But memory has huge significance in everyday life, as those who have poor memories will testify. If we forget what we have heard, seen or experienced this reduces our efficiency dramatically. In ancient times, a good memory was a vital piece of survival equipment, warning of previous dangers and experiences, or remembering routes and pathways. There are many books written about how to develop and keep your memory as it has such an impact on our functioning.

Fine Motor Control

In an academic context, this is simply the ability to manipulate writing tools effectively. In a wider sense, good fine motor skills are required for all activities which involve us using our hands, from dressing oneself to unlocking a door, using the telephone, switching on a lamp and so on. Underdeveloped fine motor skills will hinder literacy because the child will feel insecure in his ability to put pen to paper and in the resulting poor presentation.

Language

The importance of a child's oral language ability cannot be underestimated. Do not confuse 'language' with 'speech'. Put very simply, language is the system of communication which is internal, whilst speech is the act of speaking that language. Whilst a speech problem is instantly identifiable to all, many children mask a language difficulty because they have clear speech. Reading and writing is simply the translation of oral language into a written form. No one can put into writing, language that they do not have orally. Some may learn the technicalities of reading, but have no understanding of its meaning.

Comprehension

Comprehension, or understanding of any language, whether spoken or written, is vital for meaning to be conveyed. Without comprehension, all language is nonsense. To explain this quite clearly, have a look at the first verse of the very famous nonsense poem written by Lewis Carroll.

> '*T'was brillig and the slimy toves*
> *Did gyre and gimble in the wabe*
> *All mimsy were the borogroves*
> *And the mome raths outgrabe*'.

What does *brillig* mean? Can we tell who the *borogroves* were, or how they were feeling? How do you *gyre* and *gimble*? What is a *wabe*? These questions are not answerable, because probably only the author of the poem knew what these things were, but maybe even he didn't. To answer these questions we need to have someone explain to us what these words mean.

Some children have a poor comprehension of language or a restricted vocabulary. Returning to our imaginary Greek lesson, a good Greek teacher could teach us a thousand Greek words; some of us would remember half of them, others would remember a quarter or a third; the student with the outstanding memory might remember them all, and a few would remember only the first twenty. Children pick up a large or small vocabulary according to how much they have been taught at home and at school, how wide their experience has been and how good their understanding and memory are.

Here again, much can be done by parents talking, listening, teaching and explaining to their children the meaning of new words, ideas and concepts, as they come across them. The art of conversation is extremely important.

Recognising Difficulties

Much can be learnt about a child's sub-skills or lack of sub-skills through careful observation by an attentive parent. Here are some signs to watch out for:

- A poor memory is very quickly recognised! The child who forgets instructions, who cannot recite rhymes and poems easily and forgets people's names, may be showing signs of a poor auditory memory. If he forgets what he saw in a picture book for example, then his visual memory may be weak. A child who finds reciting the months of the year or the order of the seasons may have problems with his sequential memory.

- Visual discrimination difficulties can be spotted in the child who finds identifying shapes, colours and patterns tricky. Jigsaws might prove hard for him to complete and spotting differences between pictures isn't easy either. If a child is struggling to differentiate between a triangle and a square, then he is unlikely to be able to tell the difference between an 'a' and an 'o'.

- Many young children suffer from childhood problems such as 'glue ear', (affecting hearing), or poor articulation (affecting speech). These children should be carefully watched as their reduced hearing or sound production might hinder their auditory discrimination skills. Others who don't have these specific problems might still show signs of poor discrimination by their difficulties in playing with words; for example, with hearing the onset (i.e. the start of the word) and rhyme (i.e. the end of the word), identifying syllables and breaking compound words (e.g. 'cow - boy') up into their component parts.

- Sound blending is linked to auditory discrimination and problems are noticed in a child who cannot literally blend two or more individual phonemes together.

- Orientation problems are noticeable in a child who persists in confusing left and right after other children of his own age have achieved this. He may have difficulty placing objects the right way up and writing letters or numerals back to front. There may be poor laterality generally, i.e. right or left sidedness. Much has been written lately on the brain and laterality and it is a fascinating subject. If a child does not establish a dominant hand but rather appears to be ambidextrous, this may cause weak orientation skills generally.

- Weak fine motor skills are easily recognisable. The child will not only have difficulty holding and using writing tools, but will also find other tasks which require manual dexterity difficult. He will be the child who still needs help with buttons, belts and zips long after the other children in his age group are independent and he will struggle with construction materials and craftwork.

- Assessing comprehension and language informally can be done through listening very carefully to what the child actually says and being aware of the richness of his vocabulary. Their grammar should be noted, and *persisting immaturity* in the use of plurals, for example, 'mouses', and tenses, for example 'he goed' could be an indicator of language difficulties or delay. Do not be misled by a child who talks a lot; it is not the quantity of words but the quality which needs to be examined.

There is no doubt that as children get older such abilities and skills could be assessed much more accurately by a trained specialist such as an educational psychologist or speech and language therapist; all that we are suggesting here is that in the first instance, an observant parent can raise awareness of a child's difficulties themselves. Early identification of problems by the person who knows them best is crucial, and a child can be referred to more specialist professionals in due course if necessary. Indeed, referral, treatment and advice from outside agencies at some point might be imperative to the child's progress and should not be delayed if required. However, parents must remember that all children will develop at different rates and there is a wide range of ability which is within the norm.

If your child is already in school, and you have concerns over his progress, do talk to your child's class teacher. She is the one who will be able to allay any unnecessary anxieties on your part. Remember, she has a whole class of children the same age as your child and will know if there is a potential problem. If she agrees that there may be difficulties in any area, she will be able to investigate further.

In the first instance it is likely that she will talk with the school's Special Educational Needs Co-ordinator (SENCo). All schools have a SENCo and this is a member of staff who has an interest, training and experience in Special Educational Needs. She may be able to carry out observations or conduct specialised assessments which will help to clarify the difficulty. It is desirable and usual for the SENCo and Class Teacher to meet together with the parents to decide on a course of action. It may be that particular strategies are tried and the child's work adapted to suit his or her individual needs. The teacher may draw up a set of targets for your child which will be written down in the form of an Individual Education Plan and these will be worked on for one or two terms in order to see if this will help him make progress. If, after this, there are continued concerns by both parents and the school, the SENCo will probably refer your child to a relevant external agency; for example, a Specialist Teaching Service, Therapist or Educational Psychologist. (Each LEA will have a different structure of school support). These professionals will assess the child and advise both school and parents as to the best way forward.

Again, we must emphasise that it is important to take the advice of the professionals, and not become too anxious. Children pick up easily on their parent's worries, which is detrimental to all concerned. The teacher may feel that your child does not have a difficulty. Parents who work together with teachers make the most of their children's education.

So What Can I Do To Help My Child?

Parents can help their child by playing the games and activities suggested in 'The Fun Bit!' of this book in spare time at home.

However, be careful not to be over enthusiastic and remember that your child needs time to relax and play in other ways too. In 'The Fun Bit!' there is a range of activities or games which you can use to help strengthen the sub-skills. There is also a list of traditional games which some readers will know from their own childhood. As we said at the beginning of this book, many of these games are superb for building up the very skills which many children nowadays seem to lack. There will no doubt be some games that are familiar to you and have not been included in this book. Hopefully, with the information you have received from 'The Theory Bit!' you will be able to identify for yourselves which skills they might help, and use them to improve your child's abilities.

Unfortunately, there is no short cut to learning how to read and write, nor is there a magic cure for literacy difficulties; if there were we would not still be looking for answers to this problem in our schools. However, there are many strategies to be tried, and identifying particular weaknesses and then strengthening them through the playing of enjoyable games and activities will certainly help prepare the young child to read and write, and aid the struggling child without de-motivating him.

The Fun Bit!

We hope that by now, you will have understood and appreciate the importance of building up the skills which all children need for a successful start to literacy.

In this second section of the book, we want to be really practical and give you, the parent, a whole host of ideas for short games and activities which you can play with your child.

In the following pages there will be suggested activities suitable for use at home. These activities require a minimum of materials and equipment; indeed many of them (often the ones which build up auditory skills), require nothing at all except your voice. These ones are particularly suitable for playing in such situations as on a long car journey or while in the waiting room when visiting the doctor or dentist with either parent.

You will see that each activity is on a separate page. Beside the title we have put the symbol which shows the primary skill or skills which are practised by that particular game. If you feel that your child has a particular need to build up certain skills, then play the games which target those skills. Otherwise, play all the games as and when you want to, and you will be strengthening all the skills he needs to help build firm foundations for literacy.

Many traditional games are also excellent for strengthening certain skills; we have provided a list of these on page 85 which will give you extra ideas for activities. Parents might also welcome them as suggestions for 'stocking fillers' at Christmas time.

So Let's Get Started!

We hope that, having read through 'The Theory Bit!' you are enthusiastic about getting started and playing the games and activities with your child at home. We want both you and your child to get the most from these activities and so here are some simple reminders before you start:

- Make sure your child is calm before you begin and that you have enough time to play the game
- If you are playing at home, make sure the environment is conducive to concentration and learning; i.e. you are away from the television or computer, or brothers and sisters who may interrupt (why not ask them to join in if they can and want to?)
- Explain carefully how the game works and be prepared to have several practice tries before your child understands what is required of him
- Reward effort as well as success
- Be persistent with the activities that are difficult; these are likely to be areas of weakness
- Don't be afraid to modify games to suit your child
- Add games of your own to this bank of ideas; the more variety, the better!
- Above all, please have FUN!

List Of Activities By Primary Skill

 Visual Discrimination
Spot the Difference
Clever Card Snap!
Border Snap!
Initial Sound Snap!
Just Like Mine
Necklaces
Don't Cross the Line!
Sorting and Matching
Squiggles
Hunt the Letter!

 Memory
Tall Stories
Parrots
Copy Cat
Clever Card Pairs
Which One's Gone?
Shop 'Til You Drop!
Mobile Phone Numbers
Kim's Game

 Auditory Skills
Silly Sentences
Elephant Ears
Paint, Picasso!
Nonsense Names
Break it Up!
Bits and Pieces
I Hear with my Little Ear
Topsy Turvy Sentences
Odd One Out
Which One Doesn't Rhyme?
Clap That Word!
A Mexican Wave
Clever Cards Rhyming Lotto
Where's That Penny?
Surprise! Surprise!
Words that Don't Fit In

 Fine Motor
Mazes
Snake and Caterpillar
Make a Windmill
Make a Photo Frame

 Sequencing
Catch Me Out!
Carry On Capers!
Comic Picture Stories

Spot The Difference

The popularity of Spot the Difference puzzles continues down the generations. There is something intrinsically motivating to try and find that elusive final difference (always deliberately the hardest!). It looks as if it should be easy, but it may not be.

For children, this game builds up their visual discrimination skills in a fun way. Getting hold of some 'Spot the Difference' puzzles may not be easy; keep on the lookout for them in the children's sections of magazines and newspapers. You may find some in children's puzzle books. There is a good selection of downloadable puzzles like this on children's TV websites. However, all you really need is access to a photocopier and some correcting fluid. Find a suitable line-drawn picture in a children's colouring book or comic. Copy it twice. On one copy, using the correcting fluid, erase parts of the picture. For a child who has poor skills, or who is very young, start off by erasing whole objects, for example, a hat or a whole flower. As visual skills improve, be more selective about what to erase; maybe only one leaf or petal from the flower, or someone's watch or necklace, and so on. After you have erased the chosen parts, photocopy the erased picture a second time so that the child can not see the correcting fluid.

The advantage of 'doing it yourself' like this is that you really can adapt the level of difficulty to suit your child and then build up the complexity to provide a greater challenge!

Clever Card Snap!

Use two sets of the 'Clever Cards' (pp 68–78) to play this traditional game. You can either photocopy them or download them from the Internet, www.barringtonstoke.co.uk

This is how to make them:

Photocopy all cards twice or print them off the Internet.

To make them more interesting, colour them in if you want, but make sure you colour each pair in exactly the same colours so as not to confuse your child when they are asked to match them.

Cut the cards out carefully.

To strengthen them, either stick them onto card and cover them with sticky backed plastic, or if you have access to a laminator, use that.

Allow your child to help you to cut out and mount the 'Clever Cards', as this activity in itself will be good for improving hand/eye co-ordination and manual dexterity, thus strengthening fine motor skills.

Shuffle the cards well.

The pack is divided equally between the players and then each one takes it in turns to place a card face up in the middle of the table. Play continues this way until two identical cards happen to land one on top of the other. When this happens, the first player to shout 'Snap!' is the winner.

Border Snap!

Using the same 'Clever Cards' and the same rules, try and match NOT the main picture, but the *border*. This will be harder as it is more visually confusing and makes an excellent progression from the first game.

Initial Sound Snap!

Once again, using the same 'Clever Cards' and
the same rules, try to match cards which show
objects which start with the same sound. You
may find that this game is a little harder in the first instance, so go
very slowly at first until the child has tuned in to what is required.

While this last 'Snap!' game strengthens auditory skills, the first
two games sharpen visual skills and quick thinking, and all are
great fun!

Just Like Mine

Most children enjoy construction equipment such as Lego™, Multilink™ and so on. It is excellent for strengthening little fingers at the same time as building up thinking, visual and spatial skills. These skills can be challenged further, however, by an adult making a model first, and then asking the child to replicate it exactly, in size, shape and even colour.

The degree of complexity of the model can be adjusted to suit any level of ability, and is useful to ward off boredom at any time of the day.

It is also enormously satisfying for the child, and great fun too!

Necklaces

The aim of this game is to enable the child to replicate a pattern incorporating shape, colour and size. The skills he will use will be visual discrimination and fine motor.

You will need some laces for threading, together with an assortment of beads. Pay a visit to your local early years store where you should be able to buy a selection of large beads, laces and other items suitable for threading.

(Just a word of warning; be quite sure that your child will not be tempted to put the beads in his mouth, as he might swallow them; and do keep them out of the way of very young children.)

The adult should create a patterned necklace first of all, and give it to the child to look at. The child must then try and copy it exactly.

This activity is wonderfully versatile; if the child has a difficulty discriminating between colours, then choose beads which are the same shape but different colours; if size is a problem, keep the beads the same colour and shape but use different sizes.

Don't Cross The Line!

Below you will see a large number of symbols on the page. These can be photocopied or downloaded from the Internet, (www.barringtonstoke.co.uk). You can make them larger for those experiencing significant difficulties. There are actually two of each symbol. The child's task is to identify the pairs, then carefully, with a pencil line, join the two symbols up. The extra challenge is to try *not* to cross a line already drawn, nor to touch any other symbols except the two you are joining.

Visual perception and hand-eye co-ordination come into their own here, as do a little bit of forward thinking and mental planning.

Sorting And Matching Games

Sorting and matching games provide invaluable practice at the sub-skills for young children or those having difficulties with visual skills or language.

In nursery and early years classes, your child will have no doubt had a variety of sorting experience with cars, trains, animals, shapes, beads, bears, bricks, etc., which could be sorted into containers by colour, size, shape, purpose, or other attribute. However, for a child who is still struggling with these kinds of tasks, the more practice he can get, the better.

At home, your child may be able to sort and match various play equipment and toys that they have; in addition, they may also benefit by helping you with household tasks, e.g. sorting the laundry (whose clothes are whose?), pairing up the clean socks, putting away the knives, forks and spoons into the correct places in the drawer, putting away the shopping, i.e. sorting the dairy produce from the fruit and vegetables, and so on. For a treat, you could buy a bag of mixed sweets and enjoy sorting them out into piles before eating a few!

Squiggles

'Squiggles' is a very interactive game which most children love playing. This is because the adult has to take their turn as well. It strengthens visual skills, imagination and fine motor skills.

Begin by allowing your child to make a random squiggle on a page. It can be as complicated or as simple as he wishes, but he must NOT take his pen off the paper while making it. The adult then has to try and turn the squiggle into a drawing by adding to it as much or as little as it requires. After the child has got the idea of the game, let him try and turn one of your squiggles into a drawing. Don't worry if there seems to be a lot of monsters emerging on the paper, as long as you both have fun.

Hunt The Letter!

For this activity you will need a piece of text and several highlighter pens.

Children seem to love playing with these brightly coloured pens and will be well motivated by them to do this activity.

Find a piece of unwanted text, either a photocopied page out of a favourite book, a page from a comic or magazine, or even a sheet of newspaper. If your child is very young, then it will be a good idea to make sure that the text is big enough for him to 'read' easily.

In fact, this activity doesn't really require reading ability at all. Rather it is targeting your child's visual discrimination skills by asking him to scan lines of text for specific letters or words. Prepare him for literacy by showing him how to scan from left to right along each line of text.

If he is very young and just beginning to use these skills to discriminate letters, ask him to look for one particular letter, for example, the small letter 's' from his name, and with the highlighter pen, highlight each letter 's' he can find. You will be able to see quite easily how good he is at scanning for letters when he has finished. If he has missed any, help him find them all.

If your child has begun literacy work, ask him to look for and highlight some of our most commonly used words such as 'and', 'the', 'said', and so on.

Use different coloured highlighters to find different letters or words, and when your child has finished, he will have a very visually attractive piece of text.

Tall Stories

This exercise helps to develop a child's listening skills, concentration and memory. It needs no equipment, so like many of the auditory activities suggested in this book, is ideal when you have a few minutes to spare with the children.

The idea is to take it in turns to piece together a story. You begin by one person starting it off with the traditional, 'Once upon a time ...' and adding a sentence of their own.

For example, they might say, 'Once upon a time there was a girl.' The next person must then repeat the previous sentence and add one of their own. For example, 'Once upon a time there was a girl. She loved go-karting'. The next person could say, 'Once upon a time there was a girl. She loved go-karting. She made one out of an old pram and a dustbin lid'. The story continues in this way, with each player repeating all the previous sentences and then adding a new one of their own, until one of the players cannot remember the story or makes a mistake and has to give up.

Start off playing this game with only a few sentences. The stories can be as tall or silly as you like; the object of the exercise is to build up memory skills, and if the players have some fun along the way, so much the better!

Parrots

Give your child a selection of 'Clever Cards'.
Start off with just two or three and build up to
many more as he becomes more efficient at this
game.

Explain to him that you are going to say the cards in a particular
order and you want him to repeat the order you said and then put
the cards down on the table in the same order. In this way you can
help build up his auditory memory.

Remember that it is important to praise and reward your child for
any success. And remember too, that these little games should be
fun for you both!

Copy Cat!

You will need a piece of card, paper, or a book, in addition to two sets of 'Clever Cards', for this little memory game.

You should select three cards and place them in a line on the table in front of your child. Explain that you will let him look at the cards for a little while (approximately 5 seconds, or longer at first until he understands the game properly), and then cover the cards with the book. Now that the cards are hidden, he takes his cards and tries to reproduce the sequence in the line correctly.

When he feels he has finished, let him remove the book and see if his sequence is the same.

Start off with only two or three cards and build up to as many as the child is able.

This really tests his visual memory, which is so useful for future spelling skills.

Clever Card Pairs'

Once again bring out two sets of 'Clever Cards' for this traditional game.

Select an appropriate number of pairs of cards. You might start off with only three or four pairs (six or eight cards altogether).

Shuffle them well; then lay them out neatly face down in rows on the table in front of the child. Each player turns over two cards, placing them face up where they are on the table so all players can see. If they are the same, the successful player keeps that pair and wins another go. The player who manages to turn up the most pairs of cards is the winner.

This is a brilliant game of visual memory; as the child improves his skills, you can use more pairs of cards.

Which One's Gone?

Bring out the 'Clever Cards' for this visual memory game.

Lay down three cards face up on the table in front of the child.

Allow him to look at them for approximately 5 seconds. He then has to close his eyes and turn away while you remove one of them. When he turns back and looks at the cards again, ask him 'Which one's gone?' He must try and remember which one has been removed.

Start off by leaving all the cards exactly where they were, including the gap where the missing card was. This will help his memory at first. As the child gets better at this game, keep the remaining cards in the same order, but close the gap. This means he will not be getting a clue from the positioning. Finally, you can remove the card and then jumble up the remaining cards; quite difficult, especially if you increase the challenge by working up to five or six cards.

Have a go at this one yourself!

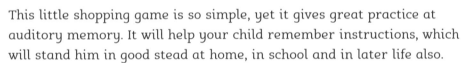

Shop 'Til You Drop!

If Britain is a nation of shopkeepers, perhaps that's why so many of our children love to pretend to play at shops.

This little shopping game is so simple, yet it gives great practice at auditory memory. It will help your child remember instructions, which will stand him in good stead at home, in school and in later life also.

Give your child a shopping bag or basket of some kind. You will also need to find a selection of items to be shopped for; in early years stores you can buy plastic fruits, vegetables and groceries, or more cheaply you can use real produce and tins from the kitchen cupboards.

Allow the child to set out their 'stall' and then go and sit away from it. The reason for this is so that time will elapse as the child crosses the room to 'buy' his shopping, which will better test his memory. Ask him to go and buy you, for example, an apple, a carrot and a packet of crisps. He should then go across to the stall and choose the correct ones to put in his basket and bring back to you. Clearly, you can start off with just one or two items and build up to as many as the child can manage. As he gets better at playing this game, tell him you are going to ask him to wait until you count to five before he can go and buy his shopping. This will challenge his memory, as he will have to hold the information in his head for longer.

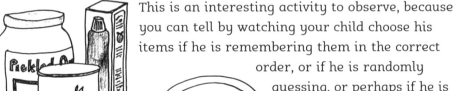

This is an interesting activity to observe, because you can tell by watching your child choose his items if he is remembering them in the correct order, or if he is randomly guessing, or perhaps if he is repeating the list back to himself. Maybe he will always remember only the last thing you asked for. This will give you reasons perhaps as to why he may have difficulties at home or in school with following instructions. It may also hint at his preferred way of remembering things, e.g. by repeating them verbally.

Mobile Phone Numbers

A few years ago, this activity would
have only been suitable for teenagers.

However, with the number of Primary age children now
owning a mobile phone increasing rapidly, (and those who
currently don't, wishing that they did), it is suitable for
almost all but the youngest children.

It is another exercise to build up auditory memory skills,
which once again will help children to remember what
they have heard or been told verbally in school, at home or
anywhere else. Good auditory memory is so vital for
academic success as much of our school curriculum is taught in an
auditory way, and increasingly so as children move up the school. It
reaches its climax in academic institutions such as universities where
staff deliver lectures to a large number of students in a large
auditorium.

Explain that you are going to tell the child a phone number, and they
must try and write it down in their telephone notebook or on a piece of
paper. Start off where the child is at; e.g. if they can only remember two
numbers, then start from there and build up the numbers as they
improve. When they are confident with several numbers, you may then
like to challenge him to write down the numbers *in reverse order*. This
is a much harder task – try it yourself – and means you have to store
information much more securely in your short-term memory. If the
child is successful at this latter challenge, he is doing really well.

In order to play 'Mobile Phone Numbers' at all, the child must have a
sound knowledge of numerals zero to nine and the ability to write them
confidently.

Elephant Ears

This is a game to encourage concentration and listening skills. It can be played at home, especially if you have a time set aside for stories. The aim is to encourage your child to listen very carefully for a particular word within a story. For this reason, it is a good idea to choose a story that the child is familiar with, so they can concentrate on listening out for the word and not get engrossed in the meaning of a story which is new to them. (It would be difficult to do both tasks at the same time.)

Choose, for example, a familiar story which contains a lot of repeated phrases; fairy tales fit the bill nicely. Let's use, for example, the 'Three Billy Goats Gruff'. Explain to your child that you are going to read a favourite story. You want them to listen ever so carefully for a special word, for example in this story, 'troll' or 'bridge'. (These words will occur several times in the story.) Each time they hear you say that special word, they can clap their hands, or say 'Gotcha!' or some other appropriate response.

Your child will have fun trying to catch you out and you will be able to ascertain how well he is concentrating and listening to what you are saying.

Paint, Picasso!

This is an exercise which teaches the child to listen very carefully to auditory instructions. It does not matter whether or not he has completed a painted masterpiece! You will be able to tell how much and how well he has listened to what

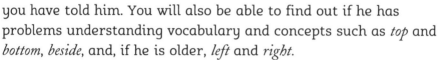

you have told him. You will also be able to find out if he has problems understanding vocabulary and concepts such as *top* and *bottom*, *beside*, and, if he is older, *left* and *right*.

Make sure your child has good quality paints, felt pens or crayons. There is nothing more demoralising for all of us than to try and do a good job with poor equipment and tools.

Simply instruct your child to draw, or paint, exactly what you tell him to. If there is more than one child playing, maybe a brother, sister or friend, you can tell them that you can compare finished paintings and see how similar they are. If they have ALL been listening carefully, their pictures should all look the same. To encourage a reluctant child, try and make use of his particular interests; for example, if he loves cars, describe a scene where there is a red Mercedes parked on a road beside a blue Jaguar.

If you are having difficulty thinking of something, here is one to get you started:

'Draw me a hill with a house on the top. The house has five windows. It has a green front door with a black, round door knob. Outside the house is a tall tree, and underneath the tree is a swing. A dog is running down the hill'. And so on.

Adapt the level of difficulty to suit your child. For a child who finds auditory processing difficult, give him only one element of the picture at a time; then as the child improves, increase the complexity and give him two or more instructions together.

Nonsense Names!

This is another little game that you could play for a few minutes every now and again when you have some spare time; maybe in a traffic jam on the way to the supermarket. It is again building up those all-important phonological skills; hearing sounds and playing around with them in a fun way.

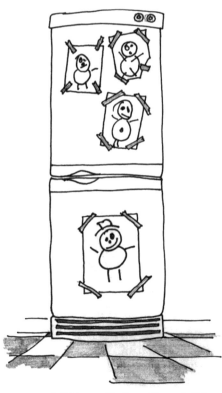

Nonsense Names! helps the child to focus on the initial sounds.

Ask your child to try and think up some funny names which have one or two funny adjectives preceding them. All the elements of the names must begin with the same letter!

Examples might be: Jolly Jumping Jane; Helpful Harry; Big Bad Ben; Running Robert; Choosy Charles; and so on. The names can be a funny as you like; the object is to concentrate on the initial sound of each word.

To extend this activity, the child might like to draw pictures of these characters, and they could be displayed in a 'Rogues Gallery!' They could even go on to tell a story about the adventures of these fictitious characters together with you at storytime or bedtime.

Break It Up!

This is another very important little game for developing phonological awareness. It encourages the child to listen very carefully to the COMPONENT PARTS of words. Being able to do this orally is the foundation for being able to do this in writing; spelling is all about breaking words up into parts orally, remembering how to spell those parts and then joining or blending them back together to make a written word.

'Break it up!' is played orally, and needs no equipment, so is an ideal game to be played in a few free minutes at home or in a waiting room. You just need to have a good supply of compound words to say to the child. Here is how you play it, together with a list of words to get you started:

Tell your child that you are going to say a word. Then you are going to ask him to tell you what the word would sound like if it had a bit missing.

For example,

Listen to the word 'dragonfly'. If I take away 'fly', what am I left with? The child should answer, 'dragon'. Or, listen to the word 'classroom'. If I take away 'class', which part is left? And so on.

Here are some more …

Lighthouse	Superman	Headlight
Cowboy	Supermarket	Firefly
Moonlight	Superstore	Butterfly
Ladybird	Batman	Buttercup
Milkman	Seaside	Housework
Treetop	Flowerpot	Football
Horseshoe	Spotlight	Outside
Timetable	Snowman	Greenhouse
Showdown	Snowflake	Cornflake
Cornflour	Hazlenut	Pineapple

This is really worth practising until the child is proficient, as it will help him to progress onto breaking words down into even smaller chunks.

Bits And Pieces

This game follows on from 'Break it up!' where we were encouraging the child to learn how to break compound words up into two component parts orally. If your child is still struggling with 'Break it up!' then he is probably going to find this game too difficult; give him more opportunities to play 'Break it up!' instead.

Say a word for your child, for example, 'cart'. Now tell him that you want him to say the word again, but this time you want him to leave the end *sound* off, i.e. the 't'. He should say 'car'. You might have to practise this a few times until he gets used to it, so here are some more words to get you started:

Fork (*for*)	Sandy (*sand*)	Plate (*play*)
Boat (*bow*)	Wind (*win*)	Plump (*plum*)
Mist (*miss*)	Sword (*sore*)	Bored (*bore*)
Grown (*grow*)	Treat (*tree*)	Dent (*den*)
Slope (*slow*)	Graze (*grey*)	Goat (*go*)
Time (*tie*)	Pinch (*pin*)	Bite (*by*)

Now you can ask him to say a word with the first sound left off. Here are some words:

Slow (*low*)	Start (*tart*)	Great (*rate*)
Grime (*rhyme*)	Feel (*eel*)	Cup (*up*)
Bend (*end*)	Snail (*nail*)	Break (*rake*)
Stop (*top*)	Buy (*eye*)	Fruit (*root*)
Creep (*reap*)	Trail (*rail*)	Broom (*room*)
Sweep (*weep*)	Grain (*rain*)	Brush (*rush*)
Flop (*lop*)	Trot (*rot*)	Part (*art*)

Do remember that you are asking him to leave off the sound, and not the letter, e.g. with the word slope, leave off the final 'p' sound, not the letter 'e'.

I Hear With My Little Ear

This game is ideal for a boring car journey as no materials are required. We have seen how important phonological awareness is if a good foundation is to be built for literacy. Recognising rhyme and playing around with rhyming words are essential but can also be highly entertaining.

This little game is similar to the traditional game of 'I Spy'.

The adult says: 'I hear with my little ear, something which rhymes with ....' and then has to say a word. Start it off simply at first until the child has got used to it. So you might begin with a simple word like 'cat'. The child has to say a word that rhymes with it; so 'bat', 'fat', 'rat', etc. are all acceptable. At this very early stage, don't worry if your child gives a word which doesn't have the same spelling; as long as they SOUND the same, it's O.K. At a much later stage in literacy you can introduce the different ways we have in English of spelling the same sounds. So, for example, if you ask for a word that rhymes with 'meat', and they say 'feet', that's a good response.

Have fun!

Topsy Turvy Sentences

This is a good auditory exercise which requires no materials, just good listening skills. You could play it on an uneventful rainy day or while waiting at the bus stop.

Say a sentence in which some or all of the words are in the wrong order. See if your child can unjumble the words and then repeat it back to you correctly!

Sometimes thinking of such sentences is difficult, so here are some to get you started. The first ones are easy, and have only one word in the wrong place. They can get progressively harder and harder. To be successful, the child must develop a good short-term working memory and knowledge of sentence structure.

Have a go with these, and then you can think of others when you have found the right level of difficulty for your child:

Hens eggs lay.
Chocolate I like.
The cat on the mat sat.
The boy crying was.
They park went to play in the.
Rabbits have tails fluffy.
Snow cold is.
Clowns laugh make me.
I like to the cinema going.
I Mum love my.

You can extend this activity for a child who is already reading and writing in two ways; firstly, you can write out the words on separate pieces of paper, jumble the pieces up and then ask the child to rearrange them in the correct order. Or, secondly, you can write the jumbled up sentence out on a piece of paper and ask him to re-write it underneath in the correct order.

Odd One Out!

Most children enjoy the rhythm of a little rhyme, and so they will hopefully enjoy this activity. The purpose of 'Odd One Out!' is to encourage careful listening to the initial or final sounds of a word. This is one of the earliest steps in learning to read.

Here's the rhyme:

'I won't whisper, I won't shout,
Can you hear the odd one out?'

This little rhyme precedes the saying of a set of three simple words, two of which have the same initial sound. The child has to discriminate which word starts with a different sound and tell you. Once they become used to this and begin to get them correct, allow the child to say the rhyme and test you! This will give them practice at using their discrimination skills the other way, which will help them with spelling in the future.

You can then go on to ask them to hear the odd one out from a group of three words of which two have the same END sound and one is different.

Here are some groups of words to get you started!

Initial sounds:	Final sounds:
dog, dice, pen (odd one out is pen)	get, pit, man (odd one out is man)
like, house, lift	so, me, go
flower, top, tractor	clap, bed, lip
horse, car, happy	ham, rag, leg
monkey, meat, nose	garden, window, train
bag, sand, soup … and so on!	rope, miss, map … and so on!

Which One Doesn't Rhyme?

This little game is one to play in the car on a long journey, and is similar to 'Odd One Out!'. In that game we were concentrating on helping the child hear the initial and final sounds of a word.

In 'Which One Doesn't Rhyme?' you play the game in exactly the same way, but the child is listening for the word that *doesn't* rhyme with the other two.

As we said previously, children enjoy the rhythm of a little rhyme, and so this time, you can start off each turn with the words;

'Listen carefully all the time,
And say the word which doesn't rhyme!'

Then continue to play by saying three words, two of which rhyme, and one which doesn't. The child has to tell you which word that is.

Once again, here are some groups of words to get you started, but in fact, the list is endless. You will see that they get harder as the list goes on, because we are introducing elements which may confuse a child. Keep using very simple ones at first until the child is confident, and then increase the difficulty gradually.

mouse, tin, house	green, been, sky
hot, grow, mow	fun, lit, gun
tell, well, star	black, fight, light
flower, shop, shower	trick, tree, brick
lady, baby, maybe	under, umbrella, thunder
cream, dream, crumb	tough, toffee, enough

Clap That Word!

Here is a game which will teach 'syllabification', i.e. being able to hear the syllables within a word. This is a very important skill, because it helps us to break words up into manageable 'chunks' when we are reading something unfamiliar. Likewise, when we are attempting to spell a difficult word, spelling small chunks and then piecing them together helps us build up the whole word.

It will also teach your child to concentrate and listen carefully.

Don't be afraid to teach the word 'syllable' to the child; it will help him throughout his school life if he understands the terminology which will be used in Literacy.

Start off from where the child is by clapping out the syllables in his name. If it is 'Jack', then one clap will be required. If it is 'David', then it will be two, three for 'Christopher' and so on. Say the word as you clap. Get the child to do the same, and try several names of friends and family until he can do it confidently. Now move on to clapping out the syllables in many different words, simple or complex, depending on how easily the child is learning. You can eventually ask him to tell you *how many* syllables are in the words, and at this point he may be able to leave out the actual clapping and work it out in his head.

This activity also paves the way for the future when the child will be learning groups of words which share the same spelling pattern.

Note: If the child seems to persist in having difficulty identifying the correct number of syllables, ask him to rest his chin on the top of his hand so that when he says a word he can count how many times his chin drops and feel how many syllables there are.

Mexican Waves ... And Other Stories!

The following activities are best done with more than one person. At home, however, either parent could easily do the storytelling part with one or two brothers, sisters or friends as participants.

Seat everyone taking part in a circle. Explain to them that you are going to make an action, and you want each one of them in turn, going round the circle, to copy your action.

For example, you might begin by the traditional Mexican Wave action of raising both hands and arms up and over your head and back down again. Each participant in turn has to copy this action; the beauty of the wave effect being achieved by the close timing of each person's action following on from the one before. You can try any kind of action, large movements such as jumping up, twirling round, making a star shape with arms and legs, curling up into a ball, or smaller movements such as clicking fingers, clapping, blinking, shaking heads, and so on.

The purpose is to encourage concentration and imitation of motor skills.

This activity can be extended to include sound effects for stories, which requires both listening and concentration skills, and promotes the imagination. For example, the adult will tell a story (which they can make up as they go along), and when they come to a part in the storyline where they need a sound effect, the leader makes it, copied immediately by the other participants. This is great fun, and an excellent way to engage a child or group of children in listening carefully to a story.

On the next page, we have included a story as an example to get you started. The words in italics need to be acted or sounded out to the best of your imagination.

'A Trip to the Seaside'

'The children woke up sleepily, *rubbed their eyes, stretched their arms and yawned*. Then they remembered that today they were going to the seaside. They packed their lunch box with goodies, (*yum, yum*), and got on the bus. The bus went chugging along the road, while the children *all bumped up and down in their seats*.

At last they arrived at the seaside. Everybody *jumped* out and *ran* onto the beach. The sand *scrunched* under their feet and the *roar* of the *waves* was deafening. They made mud pies and sand castles. They paddled in the water, *splish, splash*! What fun they had!

After lunch, the sky turned dark. It looked like it might rain. It began to get cold and the children *shivered*. *Brrrrr*! The wind started to howl. Everyone packed up their things in a hurry. They rushed back to the bus, just as the first drops of rain began to fall. *Pitter, patter. Pitter, patter.* Soon, the sound of the rain was *beating* on the roof of the bus, and the children decided to sing out loud to drown the noise.

What do you think they sang?

Yes!

'The Wheels on the Bus go Round and Round …'

Words That Don't Fit In!

This little listening game helps a child's understanding of words, helps him to put words into categories, and at the same time, sharpens up his short-term memory. All in all, a very useful way to spend a few spare minutes.

The adult should explain that she is going to say three words. Two of the words have something in common. One of the words is *not* like the other two. Your child has to tell you which one doesn't fit in with the others.

Let's take an example; Mum or Dad says, 'Cow, train, dog'. At first it will be a good idea to discuss the words with the child pointing out common features. Talk about the fact that a cow and a dog are both animals, and that people look after animals. They both have four legs and a tail. And so on. Now point out that trains are not animals; they are machines, that people can ride in them or drive them. Also, they are made out of metal.

Explain then that in this instance, 'train' is the word which doesn't fit in with the others.

Here are some more ideas to get you started:

- daisy, rose, television
- doll, coat, jumper
- sausage, elephant, cake
- plate, spider, fly
- car, book, aeroplane
- puppy, kitten, bucket
- pencil, paintbrush, chair, pen
- fish, whale, crab, camel
- butterfly, boat, wasp, bee, moth
- cupboard, bed, snow, table, desk

Once your child has grasped the idea of putting words into categories and finding ones which don't fit in, you can make it harder so he has to think more carefully about the categories! Try ones like:

- pear, banana, orange, fishcake (you can eat them all, but one is *not* a fruit), and so on!

Your child may have ideas of his own about alternative categories, and if he can explain *why* they go together, that's fine.

Surprise, Surprise!

This is a simpler version of the traditional game, Animal, Vegetable, Mineral, and more suitable for the younger or less able child. The adult should have a special little 'surprise' box, into which they can pop a small object. This adds motivation to the game, because we all know that children love boxes.

It is a game of deduction, whereby the adult places an object into the box and encourages the child or children to ask questions to see if they can find out what is inside. For example, the adult might put a pencil sharpener inside the box, provoking such questions as, 'Is it used in school?' 'Is it something all the children use?' 'Can you eat it?', 'Does it make a noise?' and so on. The questions must be 'closed' questions, that is, questions which can only be answered by a 'yes' or a 'no'.

As well as exercising their questioning skills, they also have to think carefully and by a process of elimination they will eventually succeed in discovering what's inside.

As the child becomes better at this game, the adult can put something imaginary into the box, (such as an elephant!), which, needless to say, will greatly widen the scope for richer and more varied language.

'Where's That Penny?

This fun activity can be easily played at home with either parent. It is a good one to aid the development of language and in particular, questions and concepts.

The adult needs to choose an object to hide. If your child has a favourite tiny toy or trinket which can be easily hidden, by all means use that. If not, use a shiny penny as suggested here.

The game is played simply as follows; the child closes their eyes while the adult hides the penny somewhere out of sight in the room. By asking a battery of questions, the child has to find out exactly where the penny is. For example, questions such as 'Is it by the window?' or, 'Is it behind the doll's house?' are asked to locate it. The adult responds by saying simply 'yes' or 'no'. They cannot get up and look for it; rather they must find it only using language. To help the child, it is permissible for the adult to tell the child when they are getting close. They could also use responses such as 'You're getting hotter' or, 'No, you're very cold' to indicate how close the child is to finding the penny.

By hiding it in different places, you can encourage the correct use of concepts such as 'behind', 'on', 'in', 'on top of', 'next to', 'underneath', 'beside', 'below' and so on.

When the child has got used to playing the game, allow them to be the one to hide the penny; Mum or Dad can ask the questions which will challenge their child's understanding.

Have fun!

Mazes

Drawing along maze paths is great fun for children, strengthening visual skills, forward planning and fine motor skills (pencil control). You can buy books of mazes for children to complete, or you can draw your own for him. Here is an example of one for you to photocopy or download and try with your child ....

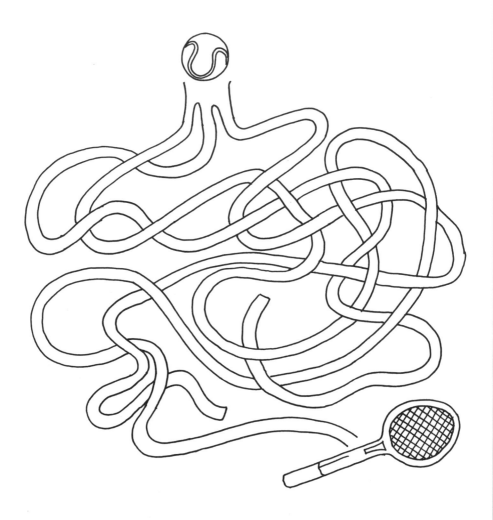

Caterpillar and Snake

Craftwork is particularly good for developing fine motor skills. On pages 59–63 you will find a selection of activities for you and your child to do together to promote manual dexterity.

1. Photocopy or download, cut out and colour

2. Accordian fold your Caterpillar or Snake

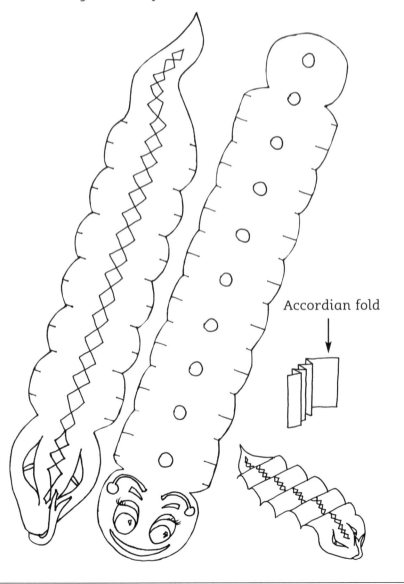

Accordian fold

Make a Windmill

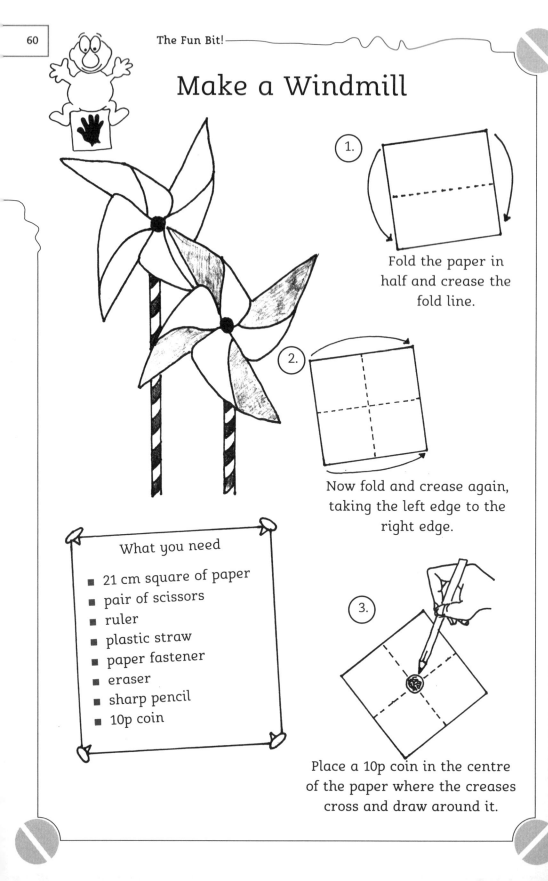

1. Fold the paper in half and crease the fold line.

2. Now fold and crease again, taking the left edge to the right edge.

What you need

- 21 cm square of paper
- pair of scissors
- ruler
- plastic straw
- paper fastener
- eraser
- sharp pencil
- 10p coin

3. Place a 10p coin in the centre of the paper where the creases cross and draw around it.

4.
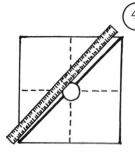

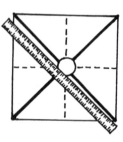
Use a ruler to draw a diagonal line from corner to corner. Stop the line when you get to the circle.

5.
Cut along the lines. (Don't cut into the circle.)
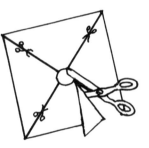

6.
Cut 5 mm off the end of the straw.

7.
Using the point of the pencil and the eraser, make a hole at one end of the straw.

The sail is made by folding a corner of each triangle to the centre.

8.

Sails

Short piece of straw

9.

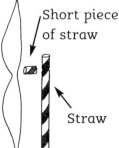

Paper fastener

Straw

Construct your windmill using the diagram above. Pass the paper fastener through the sails, 5 mm straw and long straw and open it out – HAVE FUN!

Make a Photo Frame

1. You will need a square sheet of paper approx 21 cm × 21 cm or bigger. Ribbon, sticky tape and some pens or pencils to decorate.

2. 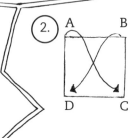 Fold your paper so that corner A meets corner C and then open flat. Now fold so that corner B meets corner D and open flat again.

You should now have two creases as shown by the dotted lines on this diagram

3. The point where the creases cross is called the centre point. All four corners A, B, C and D are to be folded one by one so that they meet at the centre point.

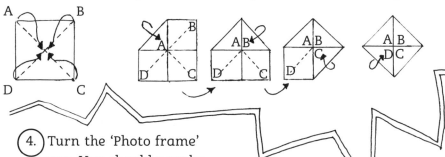

4. Turn the 'Photo frame' over. You should now be unable to see any of the corners A, B, C or D.

Your 'Photo frame' should look like this with the creases shown by the dotted lines on this diagram.

5. All four corners E, F, G and H are to be folded one by one so that they meet at the centre point.

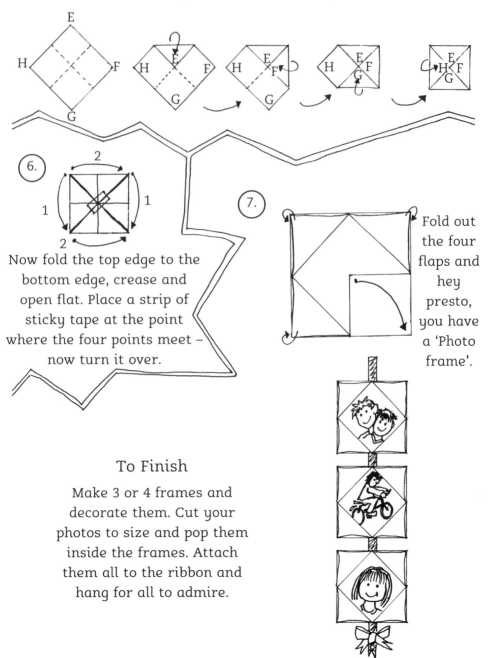

6. Now fold the top edge to the bottom edge, crease and open flat. Place a strip of sticky tape at the point where the four points meet – now turn it over.

7. Fold out the four flaps and hey presto, you have a 'Photo frame'.

To Finish

Make 3 or 4 frames and decorate them. Cut your photos to size and pop them inside the frames. Attach them all to the ribbon and hang for all to admire.

Carry On Capers!

This activity is based around copying and making patterns. As we saw in 'The Theory Bit!' sequencing skills and sequential memory underpin many aspects of literacy, and both making and identifying patterns is a good place to start. It can also be colourful, creative and fun!

You will need:

A variety of equipment such as pegboards and pegs, gummed shapes, beads, rubber stamps, crayons, paper and so on. You will find household items such as coloured clothes pegs, socks or Smarties equally useful.

Begin by making a pattern yourself, simple at first, (e.g. one with perhaps only two components in it), and then ask the child to copy it.

Then ask him to continue it.

Or show him a pattern that you have already made and ask him to say what it is, e.g. pink peg, red peg, blue peg, pink peg, red peg, blue peg, and so on. By verbalising it in this way he is embedding the repeated aspect of patterning in his auditory memory.

Encourage him to make his own patterns either with the equipment or with crayons and paper. He could maybe decorate a picture with a patterned border; if someone is having a birthday, then he could try making a patterned necklace from different shaped or coloured beads.

For further variety, draw a pattern on a snake, or train, a kite string or other favourite object.

Whatever you do, use plenty of bright and colourful materials, and have fun!

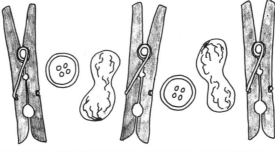

Comic Picture Stories

Sequencing pictures to tell a story is very good for future creative writing. Children need to grasp the fact that stories and books have a beginning, middle and an end. They need to understand that stories mirror what goes on in real life and are also bound by time. Events have a sequence and for a story to make sense, the sequence has to be correct.

You can purchase sets of picture cards which depict storylines through educational suppliers. However, a cheaper option could be to buy a simple and well illustrated children's comic, cut out a sequence of pictures, and ask the child to put them into order so they tell the story. You can read the story to him a few times if he finds this difficult and do not hesitate to help him if he needs it. You could then help him to make it into a little book by sticking each picture onto a separate piece of card, then binding them all together with ribbon or string.

Another similar activity could be for the child, together with the adult, to make up a story, draw pictures to illustrate various parts of the story, and then put them into correct sequence and make it into a little book as before.

In addition to practising sequence, by making his own books, this activity will also be encouraging the child to have confidence with creative writing, together with a respect for and a love of books.

You could use the books as gifts for other members of the family.

Catch Me Out!

As we said in the first section of this book, the ability to sequence is a very important skill for literacy, especially spelling. If a child has poor sequencing skills when young, for example, they cannot correctly recite simple, well known sequences such as the days of the week, months of the year or the order of the seasons, then this may indicate that they might have spelling difficulties later on.

To play 'Catch Me Out!' recite a sequence but MISS OUT one or two elements; for example, recite the months, but miss out May and October. Or try the days of the week, missing out Wednesday. If your child can count to ten, recite them for him but miss out the number 7. See if he can spot which ones you have left out!

If that exercise is too difficult, try reciting a simple song or rhyme which the child knows well, and sing it missing out a particular word. For example,

'The wheels on the ... go round and round,' etc. This will get them used to listening for something missing and will also give them practice at concentrating.

Clever Cards

Several very useful games in this book require the 'Clever Cards'. Some games will require two sets. This is how to make them.

1. Photocopy all cards twice or download them, www.barringtonstoke.co.uk.

2. To make them more interesting, colour them in if you want, but make sure you colour each pair in exactly the same colours so as not to confuse your child when they are asked to match them.

3. To strengthen them, either stick them onto card and cover them sticky backed plastic, or if you have access to a laminator, use that.

Clever Cards

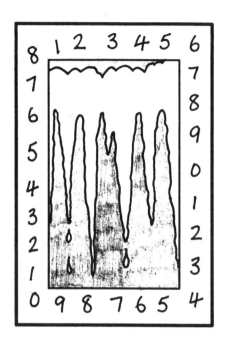

Clever Cards

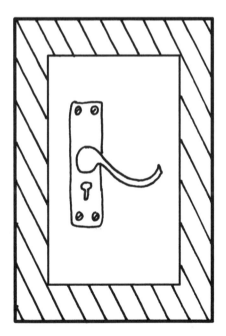

Clever Cards

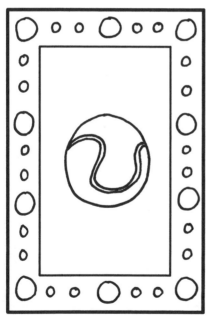

Clever Cards

Clever Cards

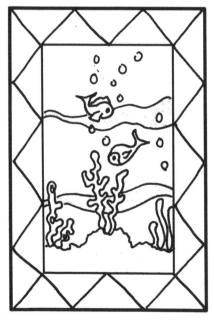

Clever Cards

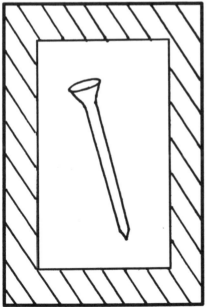

Clever Cards

Clever Cards

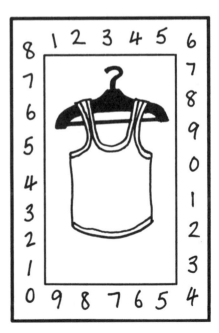

Clever Cards

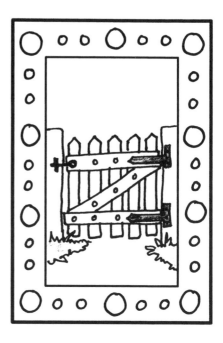

Clever Cards

Clever Cards

Clever Cards Rhyming Lotto

Use the five lotto boards which you will find on pages 80–84. To make the boards, as with the Clever Cards themselves, you can either photocopy them or download them from the website, then mount them onto cardboard and cover them with sticky backed plastic, or else laminate the boards if you have access to a laminating machine. By doing this, you will strengthen the boards so that they will last longer.

Although you can easily play this game with your child alone, we have included three extra boards in case you wish to play as a family with brothers and sisters or friends.

You will need to select the matching rhyme card for each picture on the boards being used before you begin. So if you are just using two boards, select the eight rhyming cards. If you are using all five boards, find the twenty cards which rhyme. (These will be: map, goat, fire, date, pen, ball, bicycle, rat, nest, candle, lion, hand, tree, van, sea, king, log, hut, nail, fan.)

Each player has a lotto board. Shuffle the selected Clever Cards and place in a pile in the middle of the table.

Each player in turn picks up the top card from the pile and everyone has to look and see if they have the picture on their board which rhymes with it. The player who has this takes the card and places it on his board on top of the picture it rhymes with. The first player to complete his board is the winner. (If there are only two players, each one can have two boards to make the game more difficult.)

A slightly harder version of this can be played in the following way with a pile of coins or counters. Each player in turn chooses a picture on his lotto board and then has to say as many words as possible which rhyme with it. He can place one coin or counter on the picture for each word he thinks of. Continue round all the players until everyone has had a go with each of their four pictures on their board. The player who has collected the most coins or counters is the winner!

Rhyming Lotto   Board 1

Board 2

Board 3

Board 4

Board 5

Traditional Games

Here is a list of traditional games – great as stocking fillers or pocket money games!

Jacks   *Fine Motor Skills*

'Cat's Cradle Games'   *Fine Motor Skills*

'Pick-a-Stick' (Mikado)   *Fine Motor Skills*

'Where's Wally?' books   *Visual Discrimination*

Marbles   *Visual & Fine Motor*

Dominoes   *Visual & Fine Motor*

Tiddlywinks   *Visual & Fine Motor*

Jigsaws   *Visual, Orientation & Fine Motor*

Construction equipment   *Fine Motor*

A variety of card games such as:

- Old Maid   *All good for thinking skills generally*

- Donkey

- Happy Families

- Trumps

There is a huge range of puzzles on the market which help children's visual, thinking and fine motor skills. Take a look in good toyshops or browse the Internet for good toy, game and puzzle websites.

There are, of course, many other ways to help prepare your child for literacy. In this book we have concentrated on boosting the mechanical processes required for reading, spelling and writing. However, there are other ways in which parents can help foster motivation for literacy and build up skills. Finally, then, these are our 'Top Tips':

- Talk and listen to your child – develop the art of conversation with them from an early age.

- Read stories and surround them with books. Show by your example that you enjoy reading too.

- Always take the time to explain things or words to them.

- Point out words in the environment to show that written words have meaning.

- Play with words orally.

- Read poems and rhymes; children seem to love these.

- Help fine motor skills by practising with buttons, bows, zips, etc.

- Use the best quality materials, writing tools, paper, etc. that you can find.

- Encourage plenty of physical activity, give your child lots of love, and do have fun together!

A Word for Parents of Older Children Who are Struggling to Read

For the younger child, there is a wealth of simple reading books on the market which are written with the younger age group in mind. Start off with picture books that have colourful illustrations and a lot of repetition in the story. Many fairy tales and other traditional stories are ideal for this.

If your child is in the early years of his school life, no doubt he will be bringing appropriate books home to read with you.

However, if your child is older, yet is continuing to struggle with reading for whatever reason, it can become difficult to find appropriate reading material for him. He cannot be expected to continue to want to read books containing subject matter which he may find too childish. He needs books that have age appropriate storylines but contain simple text at a level he can read. This will encourage him to continue reading and give him a taste of success.

Barrington Stoke has published a range of titles which meet this need and prove very popular with the reluctant reader. They commission first-class children's authors to write short action-packed fiction. The manuscripts are then edited by child editors (consultants), who highlight words they cannot read, pick out archaic or overcomplicated language and comment on parts of the story they do not think work. A language specialist then collates these edits and the authors are encouraged to modify their original scripts.

At the younger level, 8–10 and 10–12, many of the titles are written at two levels. There is the standard version and a 4u2 read version. The 4u2 read version has less on the page, simpler language and speech bubbles added to the illustrations.

The books are printed on cream paper with a clear font and accessible layout.

A full range of titles can be found on their website: www.barringtonstoke.co.uk or you can order a catalogue on 0131 557 2020.

To motivate your child to read, why not ask if he can be a consultant?